Buses In Colour - Volume Four

MIDLAND RED
THE TRANSITIONAL YEARS

Les Simpson

A Nostalgia Road Publication

The **Buses in Colour** Series™

is designed and published by
Trans-Pennine Publishing Ltd.
PO Box 10, Appleby-in-Westmorland, Cumbria, CA16 6FA
Tel: +44 (0)17683 51053 - Fax: +44 (0)17683 53558

trade enquiries: www.nostalgiaroad.co.uk
personal shoppers: www.transpenninepublishing.co.uk

and printed by
Kent Valley Colour Printers Ltd.
Kendal, Cumbria +44 (0)1539 741344

ISBN 978 1903016 74 9

British Cataloguing in Publication Data
A catalogue record for this book is available from the British Library

CONTENTS

Front Cover: *This is one of the iconic BMMO CM6T/
BMMO C44Ft 'Motorway Coaches'. Registered BHA 649C,
it is seen just after arrival at Victoria Coach Station, London
off the ME1 Motorway service from Digbeth, Birmingham.*
A. L. Such/Les Simpson collection

Rear Cover Top: *Bedford SB5/Willowbrook B40F, MRF
420L was new to Harper Bros in 1974.*
Les Simpson collection

Rear Cover Bottom: *Midland Fox 2964 (OJD 414R), a
former London Transport Leyland Fleetline FE30ALR, Park
Royal H44/32F. It is seen negotiating flood waters in Cosby in
June 1983. Les Simpson collection*

Title Page: *Daimler Fleetline chassis with Alexander bodies
were one of the BMMO's first major excursions into
purchases from outside builders. Here we see 6205 (UHA
205H) in NBC 'Poppy Red' livery. Les Simpson collection*

This Page: *In all some 45 BMMO C1 chassis were built in
1948/49 with Duple C30C bodies. All were withdrawn
between 1960 and 1966., but ten saw further use (mostly for
driver training as seen here with KHA 327 leaving Nuneaton
garage. Les Simpson collection*

INTRODUCTION

Like so many schoolboys in times past, I admit to being a train spotter many years ago. As a consequence, and because I was born in Tamworth, I spent many hours in the famous station fields, just as electrics replaced steam. My spotting days were to change on the 1st August 1964, as 46245 *City of London* headed north on a Down Express.

This was also the day I was introduced to bus spotting. and following a written request to 'Midland Red' at Bearwood, I was soon in receipt of an official Fleet List booklet. At the time, the majority of the fleet were home built 'BMMO' vehicles apart from 50 Daimler Fleetline deckers and 100 Leyland Leopard saloons.

Above: *This classic view of BMMO No.5904 (PHA 504G), shows one of the company's home-grown productions a Type S22, with a BMMO DP45F body. The S22's were the last of the dual purpose BMMO line of vehicles but did not carry dual-purpose livery, being delivered in all-over red as seen here at Pool Meadow Bus Station, Coventry.*
A. L. Such / Les Simpson collection

With a 'Day Anywhere Ticket', the company's large operating area was very accessible for a young enthusiast to explore with good route coverage between the major towns and cities. The Bull Ring Bus Station in Birmingham had many routes that radiated from there bringing in vehicles from different garages.

Above: *This BMMO CM5 37-seat coach is seen in Eccleston Place, Victoria, London in the company's later plain red livery with plain upper case MIDLAND fleet name. This example was No.4817 (817 HHA).* Les Simpson Collection

Nearby was Digbeth coach station, with the added colour of BET and Tilling group coaches that broke up the dominance of Midland 'Red' and Birmingham Corporation 'blue and cream', but it was the red and black Motorway Coaches that I was most interested in.

Sadly, whilst I travelled on a majority of the stage carriage routes, I never ventured on the coach to London Victoria. It was not until March 1978 that I purchased my first 35mm camera, at which time the only BMMO vehicles left in service were S17, S21, S22, S23 and D9's .

I set about capturing as many Midland Red vehicles on slide film as I possible could, but only quite recently did I manage to secure a substantial large slide collection, from which I have ventured into this, my first picture book; hopefully illustrating the transition periods that I have experienced. The late-1960s saw the loss of the long established livery and, with the 1968 Transport Act, the formation of the National Bus Company.

With standardisation came new vehicles, while older were repainted into a corporate livery. This was followed in 1981, by a split into five smaller companies; each of which then went their own way with vehicle purchases and liveries. De-regulation came in 1986, along with major route changes and the introduction of minibuses. So, the period this book covers is mid-1960s to mid-1980s.

BRIEF HISTORY

The Birmingham & Midland Motor Omnibus Company Ltd (BMMO) was registered on 26th November 1904. From 1923 until 1970, the company designed and built most of its own vehicles. Up till 1940 it also produced vehicles for other operators. The last complete vehicle to be built was 5941 (UHA 941H) a BMMO S23, the final 50 had their bodies finished by Plaxton, 5991 (UHA 991H) being the last. The story of the company's history has been told in many previous books, and it is not intended to duplicate that work in this publication; however, it has to be said that its history as both a major fleet operator and the builder of complete vehicles, made its subsequent history a unique story and this does impact on our narration of the Transitional Years as will be seen.

Below: *In NBC Poppy Red livery, No.5407 (EHA 407D) was a BMMO D9, BMMO/Willowbrook H40/32RD. This vehicle passed to West Midlands PTE on 3rd December 1973, but it is seen in Edgbaston Street, Birmingham prior to that transfer.* A. L. Such/Les Simpson collection

MIDLAND RED SINGLE-DECKERS

The company began to produce its own vehicles at an early stage in their history, but its real development work, as far as this story goes, starts in the immediate post-World War II era. With its post-war development of both buses and coaches, the company pioneered many new innovations on the models that would still be in service during the Transitional Years. For instance, they were actually light-years ahead of the major bus firms in some respects, especially underfloor-engined models, which the majority of builders did not offer until around 1950. However, Midland Red had actually introduced its first

Above: *This is the S14 model, introduced in 1955, which were allowed to run on single rear wheels due to their low unladen weight of less than 5½ tons. Here S14, No.5718 (718 BHA) is seen outside the Lamb Inn on Market Street, Ashby-de-la-Zouch in August 1968. Les Simpson collection*

production BMMO underfloor-engined single-deckers as early as 1946, with their development coming about as a direct result of the war-time work they had undertaken in times of severe shortages of both buses and materials. The policy of self-build was perpetuated throughout the 1950s and into the 1960s, but even then the firm's works did not have the capacity to meet all of the fleet's needs.

Top Right: *In August 1961 the law allowed an increase in the length for single-deck buses and coaches from 30' to 36'. Responding to the opportunity, BMMO introduced the S16 and S17 models, both of which were 36' long. The S16 had a manual gearbox and 8-litre BMMO KL engine, the S17 had a semi-automatic gearbox with the BMMO 10.5-litre engine. Seen at Hereford garage, is No.5098 (5098 HA), a BMMO S16, and BMMO/Plaxton B52F body.*
Les Simpson collection

Below: *A later example of the S17 type is seen with No.5711 (DHA 711C), which again has a BMMO/Plaxton B52F body. It is allocated to Hartshill and working on the A1 Bromsgrove to BMC Longbridge Works service. It has the addition of a late style illuminated pay as you enter sign, and roof cantrail advertising.* A. L. Such/Les Simpson collection

Top Left: *Here we have another example of the S17 single-decker, No.5684 (CHA 684C), which was part of the second batch of 100 vehicles; these buses were fitted with drum brakes at the rear from new. Bodywork was either finished by Plaxton (Nos.5547-71) or Willowbrook (Nos.5546 & 5572-645). It is seen in the later (pre-NBC livery) though with NBC Antique Grey wheels in Wetmore Park Bus Station, Burton-on-Trent. A. L. Such/Les Simpson collection*

Below: *The BMMO S21 was designed by BMMO as a crew operated (two-man) semi-coach vehicle, for use on longer distance stage carriage services in the week and coach duties at weekends. Here No.5861 (JHA 861E) a 49-seat dual purpose coach, featuring blue vinyl high back buckets seats is seen at Shrewsbury Bus Station. A. L. Such/Les Simpson*

Above: *The Type S22 was designed for One-Man-Operation (OMO) for use on the long-distance stage-carriage services, or X services as they were otherwise known. Mechanically these were identical to the BMMO S21 and they used the 10½-litre engine coupled to a semi-automatic four-speed gearbox. Here, No.5887 (MHA 887F) is seen outside Malvern garage with the later underlined fleet name. Some vehicles carried this style of fleet name on NBC Poppy Red liveries on re-paint.*
A. L. Such/Les Simpson collection

Right : *Another example of the 45-seat dual-purpose S22 type is No.5913, (PHA 513G), which provided 45 dual-purpose seats. It is seen in plain NBC Poppy Red without white relief in Edgbaston Street, Birmingham, just after leaving the Bull Ring Bus Station.* Les Simpson

Top Left: *Midland Red took into its fleet 100 Leyland Leopard PSU3/4R chassis with either Weymann or Willowbrook BET-style bodies They entered service between December 1962 and August 1963, and were classified as LS18 or LS18A types. Designated LS18, No.5212 (5212 HA), has a Willowbrook B53F body and is seen at the Adderley Street yard, inBirmingham in un-relieved NBC livery.*
A.L.Such / Les Simpson collection

Middle Left: *By contrast, No.5184 (518 4HA) is a Leyland Leopard PSU3/4R, with a Willowbrook dual-purpose 48-seat body, and therefore originally designated LS18A. It is seen here at Swadlincote garage in October 1978, where it carries the NBC Poppy Red livery with the grey band.*
Les Simpson

Bottom Left: *Almost heresy in a Midland Red book, this picture of United Automobile's No.1600 (WHN 600M) Bristol LH6L, with an ECW B45F body may well look out of place. However, this rare scene at Rugby is explained by the fact that this bus was on hire to Midland Red from December 1974 to February 1975. This is confirmed by the lack of destination blinds on the 571 service to Daventry. Midland Red were also known to hire buses and coaches from other NCB operators to meet vehicle shortages.* Les Simpson collection.

Over the years, the company's works turned out a variety of designs following a tradition started with the first SOS buses built in 1923. In the preceding pages we have shown a selection of the vehicles that survived into the Transitional Years, but we have also shown how new types started arriving from outside sources.

The final series of single-deck buses to be built at the Midland Red's famous Carlyle Road Works at Edgbaston, Birmingham were all single-deckers. These were to three design types, including semi-coach (S21), dual purpose (S22) and service bus (S23) types. Mechanically these vehicles were similar to the earlier S17 models, but their bodies were substantially updated with longer windows and peaked front and rear roof domes. The S23 was the last type of vehicle to be designed and built by BMMO up to June 1970. The costs now outweighed the benefits, and so the S23's represented the last Midland Red built vehicles, As the company had recently been taken over by the NBC, the nationalised operation was often unfairly blamed for the end of Midland Red's unique tradition.

As will be discussed on page 24, the formation of the West Midlands Passenger Transport Executive and its implementation of a county-wide transport policy as part of local government re-organisation led to over 400 Midland Red vehicles being transferred to the new WMPTE in December 1973. This transfer included no less than 14 - S16s, 79 - S17s, eight - S21s, nine - S22s, 24 - S23s, and 80 - D9s of BMMO manufacture. There were also 136 vehicles with Daimler chassis and 52 from Leyland.

These transfers created some immediate shortages in the Midland Red fleet and a small number of vehicles were hired in from fellow NBC companies. Among the more distant ones to make the journey was a small batch from United Automobile, who were based in Darlington and covered a wide geographic territory from Yorkshire to Northumberland in the north and Cumbria in the West. Although such vehicles are not really an integral part of the Midland Red story, they are nevertheless worthy of a passing mention.

Top Right: : *Although the Midland Red company were starting to acquire its new supplies from commercial producers, No.2181, (XUX 417K) was a second-hand Ford R192 with a Plaxton Derwent II B47F body. It was acquired with the business of T. Hoggins & Sons, Wrockwardine Wood in January 1974 and seen at Worcester Bus Station.*
A. L. Such/Les Simpson collection

Middle Right: *This is fleet No.6376 (YHA 376J), Ford R192, fitted with a Plaxton Derwent II B45F. These were designated as the BMMO Type S25, and later as the F1. One hundred of these were purchased new in 1970-1 for use on the rural routes. Seen here at Shrewsbury Bus Station for the journey to Hereford via Ludlow and Leominster.*
A.L.Such/Les Simpson collection

Bottom Right: *With such a comprehensive fleet of 48- or 53-seat vehicles serving in a variety of roles, it was not surprising that further batches of Leyland Leopard chassis were acquired from 1967 onwards. This is PSU3B/4R chassis with a Marshall B53F (designated S26) and one of a batch of 13 from 1972. This one, No.6466 (DHA 466K) is seen after a heavy snowfall at Nuneaton in January 1982; complete with 'Hunter' branding. This vehicle had brown plastic seats and no power steering, they were unpopular with drivers and passengers alike.* Les Simpson

Below: *As we have already seen, Midland Red had resorted to the use of the Leyland Leopard chassis to meet its demand for various service types, and the first batch of buses based on this chassis started to arrive in 1962. We have further shown how additional batches of buses were delivered in 1967 and each year between 1971 and 1974. Here we see one of the later batches (designated S24) from 1972, No.6439 (CHA 439K). It is a Leyland Leopard PSU3A/2R with Willowbrook DP49F. When seen at Stourbridge Town station on the S53 local service, it was not looking in the least like a dual-purpose vehicle in plain Poppy Red paint.*

Although the BET style of bodywork seen on this vehicle had become very common in the NBC fleets of the early 1970s, it was a situation that was destined to change. By the end of 1974, the NBC had instructed its constituents to only buy the Leyland National for their bus operations, and from that time, the only Leyland Leopards acquired thereafter were coaches. For readers who want to know more on the development of the Leyland National, Volume Three of Buses in Colour The Leyland National *by Paul Chancellor contains numerous pictures of Midland Red National buses.*
A. L. Such/Les Simpson collection

The Ancillary Fleet

Like most bus operators, Midland Red, required a fleet of breakdown or 'service' vehicles to maintain those vehicles that encountered problems whilst out on the road. The majority of the ancillary vehicles in the fleet were converted from life-expired buses and coaches. and on this page we see just three examples. However, there were numerous applications to which old buses were put, for instance BMMO S9s and D5s were converted to tree-loppers, and BMMO D5Bs and D7s were used as mobile workshops. In the early 1970s, 11 BMMO D7's were also converted to towing vehicles. Interestingly, there were also the different styles, including one-, one-and-a-half-, two- and four-bay conversions.

Midland Red were unique amongst the larger bus operators in that they purchased Land Rovers for towing and recovery work back in the second half of the 1950s. In 1957 they loaned a short wheelbase (SWB) demonstrator from the Land Rover plant and did some simulated tows with a double-decker in tow, prior to an order being placed. A SWB model was then purchased and it was followed in 1958 by a 109" long wheelbase (LWB) Series I model with a petrol-engine and a high and low ratio gearbox, four-wheel drive, and a front-mounted capstan!

Other examples followed, and the Editor of this book tells me he recalls following one on the Wolverhampton Road (A449) towards Stourton, as it was towing an S15 single-decker towards Stourbridge. Midland Red Land Rover models are now produced by Oxford Die-Cast.

Top Right: *Here we see former fleet No.4747 (747 BHA), a D7 double-decker that was of single bay style. Converted to towing duties and wearing trade plates, it is seen in NBC livery at Tamworth Garage in December 1979.* Les Simpson

Middle Right: *Next we find former No.4531 (XHA 531), which was of the four bay style. It passed to West Midlands PTE, and is seen here recovering a BMMO D9 near Sutton Coldfield.* Les Simpson collection.

Bottom Right: *The D7's were subsequently replaced by cut-down Leyland Leopard PSU3/4R, Plaxton Panorama coaches converted for towing duties. Here we see what had been No.5830 (GHA 330D) as it rests in the yard at Nuneaton Garage in August 1980.* Les Simpson

MIDLAND RED DOUBLE-DECKERS

Although no history of the BMMO fleet should suddenly launch into a story towards its end, rather than its beginning, as far as the Transitional Years go, it is with the D9 double-decker that we must start our account. Indeed, the prototype BMMO D9 was unveiled in 1958, as a 30′ long, high-capacity double-decked bus. The BMMO had thought of building to this length as far back as 1951, but as it transpired such vehicle lengths were not legal until 1956 and it was to be three further years in the genesis. When the law changed, the firm could have simply lengthened their existing BMMO D7s, yet in view

of the developments within the single-deck fleet, a completely new vehicle was ultimately designed.

The new D9 type was fitted with a front-mounted 10.5-litre version of the BMMO KL engine, an hydraulically-operated four-speed semi-automatic gearbox, disc brakes on both axles and power steering. The front axle was independently sprung and variable rate rubber suspension was used throughout.

A further 344 'production' model D9s then entered service between January 1960 and November 1966, and with such a long production run there were inevitably many detailed changes during production. However, new styles of rear-engined front-entry buses were joining the fleet as one-man operation (OMO) increased in popularity.

Following on from a batch of 50 Daimler Fleetlines (BMMO Class DD11) delivered in 1963, Midland Red bought the Daimler Fleetline/ Alexander buses for its double-deck requirement. Before long ,149 single-door DD12s were built between 1966 and 1968. These were followed by 103 DD13s between 1969 and 1971, in double door configuration. Virtually unique to Midland Red, was the use of a two-piece flat windscreen and upper deck windows. The DD11, DD12 and LS18 classes all carried the cast BMMO badge and used the illuminated Midland sign.

Left: *This is No.4969 a BMMO D9, with a H40/32RD body, which is seen at Hereford depot. A total of 345 D9s were built, of which the prototype (No.4773) was built in 1958. The final 45 had the bodies completed by Willowbrook.*
A. L. Such/Les Simpson collection

Top Right: *At Dudley Bus Station is Fleetline CRG6LX, Alexander H44/33F (designated DD12), which was No.6060 (JHA 60E).*
A. L .Such/Les Simpson collection

Bottom Right: *Next we see one of the later Fleetline chassis, CRG6LX, Alexander H45/30D (designated DD13). The smaller lower deck capacity being due to its having a dual-door arrangement. Both vehicles carry the later pre-NBC Midland Red livery. When new, the DD12 No.6286 (YHA 286J) carried a small upper case Midland fleet name.*
A. L. Such/Les Simpson collection

All-over advertising liveries became very popular in the late-1960s and early-1970s, and it proved a very useful form of revenue when most bus companies were struggling with falling passenger numbers. Of course, this pre-dated the modern technique of vinyl wrapping and all the recipients of these adverts were then hand-painted. I remember standing for an hour watching a signwriter at his fascinating work on a D9 in Bearwood garage.

Above: *It should be pointed out that, whilst the BMMO designed and built their own chassis and bodies, some work was put out to outside contractors, a classic example being this Willowbrook-bodied D9 No.5412 (EHA 412D), which had a BMMO-designed H40/32RD body. It has been painted here in the rather gaudy, People and Postcodes advert livery for the Royal Mail.*
A. L. Such / Les Simpson collection

Top Right: *Another BMMO D9/Willowbrook combination is seen on No.5415 (EHA 415D), when it was captured on film wearing the advertising livery of Super D, the discount DIY centre of Minworth. The Super D store was actually on the 116 route between Tamworth and Birmingham, although the vehicle is seen here at the rear of Tamworth garage.*
A. L. Such/Les Simpson collection

Below: *Here we find the application of yet another hand-painted double-deck bus with over-all advertising, this time for Rediffusion, and applied at a time when colour television was still very much a product enjoyed by only the minority. The vehicle featured, No.6011 (GHA 411D), is yet another combination of the Daimler Fleetline CRG6LX chassis and the Alexander H44/33F body, which the company designated as their DD12 Type.*
A. L. Such/Les Simpson collection

DUAL-PURPOSE BUSES

Over the years, Midland Red invested in a variety of vehicles that could be equally used on stage-carriage services, coaching duties or express bus routes. These were basically bodies and chassis that were identical to standard stage-carriage vehicles, but had the internal specification and seating more usually found in coaches. The first major batch came in a 100-strong fleet of Leyland Leopard PSU3/4R chassis (5145-5244 HA) that were delivered in 1962-3, of which (25) were dual-purpose DP48Fs (LS18A). Some of these were later re-seated to become service bus variants (B53F coded LS18), like the other vehicles delivered in the 1962-3 orders. The first 25 of these Leopard chassis delivered had B53F bodies by

Weymann (5145-69) and the next had similar by Willowbrook. The next 20 had identical Willowbrook bodies with dual-purpose appointments and they featured the black-painted roofs of the coaching stock.

Another batch of ten dual-purpose PSU3/4R chassis (JHA 839-48E) were delivered with Willowbrook BET-style DP49F bodywork in 1967, whilst 52 PSU3A/4Rs entered service in 1971 (YHA 394-9J YHA 401-16J, YHA 499J and CHA 417-45K; these had destinctive leopard skin pattern moquette). A further 13 (DHA461-73K) came in 1972 and these were followed by 50 PSU3B/2Rs in 1973 (JHA199-248L). Another 50 examples of the same chassis (PHA 319-38M, SHA 639N, GJW40-9N, GOH 350-61N and GOL 362-8N) were new in 1974/5, and all had Marshall dual-purpose bodies.

Left: *Of the 550 Leyland Leopard chassis acquired by Midland Red in their designations of LS18, LA18A, LS20, S24, S26, S27 and S28, exactly half were built with bus body-work for use on stage carriage services. However, a substantial number of the others were fitted with dual-purpose seats from new. They were used on long-distance routes, with the remainder having bus seats for use on shorter, local routes. One of the dual-purpose examples No.362 (GOL 362N) was Leyland Leopard PSU3B/2R with Marshall DP49F body work. Designated Midland Red class S28, this example is seen outside the Lamb Inn, Market Street, Ashby-de-la-Zouch, the same location as S14, No.4718 earlier in the book. This picture dated May 1981. The X99 Birmingham to Nottingham service was operated jointly by Coalville and Tamworth garage.* Les Simpson

Top Right: *Designated Midland Red class S24, No.6394 (YHA 394) was a Leyland Leopard PSU3A/2R, Willowbrook DP49F. Allocated to Digbeth Depot, this one is seen at Warrington Arpley Bus Station possibly on a National Express working. The S24's carried Midland red livery, then NBC dual-purpose and finally plain NBC red.* A.L.Such / Les Simpson collection.

Middle Right: *This example was designated class C16 and this member of the class, No.366 (JOX 466P), was a Leyland Leopard PSU3C/4R with a Plaxton Supreme Express C49F body. Midland Red purchased approx 500 Leopard chassis, mainly for coach work and the longer stage carriage and X services. Seen at Shrewsbury Bus Station in April 1981 on a local service.* Les Simpson

Bottom Right: *Further Leyland Leopard chassis were given dual-purpose bodies by Willowbrook and Marshall, but 12 chassis purchased in 1980 were put in store and not bodied until 1982. By the time these vehicles were ready for delivery, the sectorisation of the company had begun and they ended up with Midland Red (Express) Limited at Digbeth, where they were used on National Express work. This is one of the 1980-built batch, which became No.796 (BVP 796V), a Leopard PSU3E/4R, with a Willowbrook 003 Express C53F body (designated CDP22). Seen at Rugeley Bus Station in November 1980 in NBC dual purpose livery. The class were to carry many liveries during their lives including Midland Express, local coach, plus after the split in 1981, many variations on local and modified liveries.* Les Simpson

Coaching Stock

As may be appreciated, Midland Red, like many of its large counterparts, ran a highly successful fleet of coaches, which it employed in a variety of duties ranging from day excursions to holiday tours, school buses to pensioners' outings, and from express services to private hire charters. Its fleet of buses and coaches was therefore varied and extensive and it included the products of its own workshops in addition to those from the specialist chassis and coach-building suppliers; indeed, Midland Red ordered quite substantial batches of vehicles for its needs.

Above: *Typifying the varied work of the Midland Red coach fleet is No.5793 (CHA 93C), Leyland Leopard PSU3/4R with a Duple Commander C49F body (designated BMMO Class LC7). Seen at Uttoxeter Races in NBC National white livery with red fleet name, it was originally delivered in the Midland Red livery with a black roof; some carried a silver fleet name. It was part of the batch (CHA 74-122C), the majority of which were sold on for further use in the early-1970s, 29 going to National Travel and six to City of Oxford. A total of nine were re-bodied by independent operators in the late 1970s, whilst No.5793 went to Black & White Motorways in 1975. A.L.Such/Les Simpson collection.*

Black and Red

I personally feel that Midland Red coaches looked their best in the black and red livery and in my days of bus spotting in the 1960s, it had plenty to influence me. The choice ranged from the BMMO's own superb 'motorway coaches' to the various types of Leyland Leopard chassis that appeared with luxury coach bodies by Plaxton of Scarborough or Duple Northern from Blackpool (the former H. V. Burlingham factory).

One of the latter offerings was a 49-strong batch of the BMMO 49-seat coaches, which came in the Midland Red coach livery of red with black roof, although these were re-painted with a maroon roof from May 1967 onwards. Some of the class were later re-trimmed and fitted with a C41F layout for 'Coach Cruise' work.

Top Right: *The BMMO CM5 coach was undoubtedly the most iconic type of vehicle ever built by any British coach operator. It was to be a ground-breaking model in many ways, and a pioneer of the 'Swinging Sixties' that lay just ahead. It owes this status to the opening of Britain's first inter-city motorway (the M1 linking Birmingham and London), on Monday 22nd November 1959. In readiness for the fast coach service that the BMMO planned to introduce on this route, they re-engineered their BMMO C5 coach design that had been introduced earlier that year. The new variant was built specifically for high-speed motorway work, and in this view we see a CM5 (826 HHA) at Blackpool.*
A. L. Such / Les Simpson collection

Middle Right: *An amalgam of a BMMO chassis and a body by an outside coach builder is seen on No.4230 (UHA 230), a BMMO CL3 with a Plaxton Panorama C36F body. Seventeen BMMO C3 chassis were re-built and re-bodied in 1962-3, and they were originally painted in a cream livery for extended coach tours, but they were put back into the traditional livery two years later.*
A. L. Such / Les Simpson collection

Bottom Right: *Designated BMMO Type LC7, and bearing Nos.5774-5822, a batch of 49 Leyland Leopard PSU3/4R chassis with Leyland O600 engine were acquired with Duple Commander C49F bodies in 1965. The LC7 class were to carry red/black, red/maroon, plain red, NBC dual purpose and National white liveries. They saw use on the joint Associated Motorways Cardiff to Birmingham service. This one, 5780 (CHA 80C) is pictured on that route whilst standing at Cardiff Bus Station.*
Les Simpson collection

National Express White

With the Transport Act in 1968, and the subsequent formation of the National Bus Company, Midland Red's identity was to become suffused into the corporate livery adopted by the nationalised concern. For its coaching and express vehicle stock, an over-all white scheme was adopted, upon which the NATIONAL name was picked out in alternating red and blue lettering, and the fleet name in red. Some of the vehicles took to the new livery quite easily, others never looked quite at home in it, especially the BMMO motorway coaches, which to many enthusiasts only ever really suited the red livery.

Top Left: *The BMMO built the prototype CM6T in 1962, but this was later re-styled with a new six-bay body, which the BMMO subsequently copied on all future designs. They then constructed a further 29 coaches at their Central Works, and these entered service between February 1965 and May 1966. This one, No.5663 (DHA 963C) is a C44F with a toilet at the rear - one of 24 so equipped. In their later years several were stored never to run again, however the others were re-styled with new additional bright work, re-trimmed seats, and large front domes and a bus style full destination board similar to the type CM6A. Seen at Nuneaton Garage. This depot operated the ME2 Nuneaton, Coventry to London service, Digbeth operated the Birmingham to London service.* Les Simpson

Middle Left: *This is No.6251 (WHA 251H), a Leyland Leopard PSU3A/4R, Plaxton Panorama C49F (designated LC11). Seen at Stechford station yard, Birmingham in October 1980, it was doing contract duties providing staff transport for British Rail track workers. It passed to Midland Red (Express) on 6th September 1981 and was one of four that were rebuilt, re-bodied with new ECW B51 C49F bodies and re-registered. All four subsequently passing to Midland Red West on 23rd December 1986.* Les Simpson

Bottom Left: *The CM6 had a very short life span and the C14 Leyland Leopard PSU3B/4RT coaches replaced the last examples of the BMMO CM6 on Motorway duties in April 1974. Here No.316 (PHA 316M) has a Plaxton Panorama Elite III C44F body. Almost identical in its location as that on the CM6T and clearly seen on the nearside is the toilet, a feature of Midland Red motorway coaches.* Les Simpson

Above: *This Leyland Leopard PSU4A/4R, Plaxton Panorama Elite C36F (designated LC10) was No.6143 (SHA 643G). Midland Red operated extended coach tours into the 1970s, with Scotland being a popular destination. The plain red livery is well illustrated with this view, as is the 'stainless steel effect' Midland Red name plate and lettering. This vehicle was not withdrawn from the fleet until December 1976. A. L. Such/Les Simpson collection*

TRANSFER TO THE WEST MIDLANDS PTE

The West Midlands Passenger Transport Executive (WMPTE) was formed on the 1st October 1969, as another consequence of the 1968 Transport Act. Then, after the Local Government Act of 1972, its main duty was to form a fully co-ordinated public transport system within the West Midlands. This become the first step in the erosion of the Midland Red 'empire' and perhaps could be described as the thin end of the wedge.

Nevertheless, on 3rd December 1973, a total of 170 stage carriage services (that were operated wholly within the new West Midlands County Council territory) transferred to the WMPTE. Along with these went a total of 413 passenger-carrying vehicles, their staff and no less than six garages; Dudley, Hartshill, Oldbury, Sheepcote Street and Sutton Coldfield. As a result, the Bromsgrove and Cradley Heath garages re-opened to provide cover for the Midland Red's cross boundary services.

Below: *Seen wearing the West Midlands logo over its original Midland Red paintwork, we find No.140, HHA 140L, Leyland National 1151/1R/2501, B52F (BMMO class N1). Passing to WMPTE when only seven-months-old, it became their No.5140 and lasted in service until 1986.*
A. L. Such / Les Simpson collection.

Above: *Again, looking distinctly out of place in any other livery but Midland Red, No.5634 (BHA 634C) is pictured at Dudley Bus Station, wearing the West Midlands PTE livery. This bus had the BMMO S17 chassis and BMMO B52F body, which was built by Plaxton. It passed to the PTE in December 1973 when it was eight-years-old, but it still retained its Midland Red number when this picture was taken.*
A. L. Such / Les Simpson collection

Right: *Former Midland Red No.107 (HHA 107L), a Leyland National 1151/1R/2501, is seen outside what had been Birmingham City Transport's Lea Hall garage in February 1981. This vehicle had been supplied by the Leyland National plant at Lillyhall in Cumbria as a 52-seater, but this capacity was reduced by one seat by the BMMO.* Les Simpson

MIDLAND RED IN THE 1970s

On 29th March 1974, the company was renamed as rgw Midland Red Omnibus Company Ltd, but the 1970s were not the best of times for public transport, as fuel prices escalated, car-ownership grew and passenger numbers shrank. To answer these problems the company commissioned Viable Network Plan in 1976, using independent consultants Colin Buchanan & Partners.

This new scheme was aimed at identifying passenger travel patterns and their requirements, and then to optimise routes and minimise the amount of vehicles to meet these needs. A trial scheme to test the concept came on 13th March 1976, with the introduction of the 'Reddibus' brand name to operate in or around Redditch.

Above: *Seen at Stratford-upon-Avon Bus Station, in May 1981 wearing the Reddibus livery was No.274 (NHA 274M), a Leyland National 1151/1R/2501 B51F.* Les Simpson

In 1977, Midland Red introduced three networks, in Evesham *Wayfarer*, Kidderminster *Wendaway* and Stratford-upon-Avon *Avonbus* with the buses being branded accordingly. This was followed in 1978 with Hereford *Wandaward* and Telford *Tellus*. Then, in 1979, Coalville and Swadlincote got *Lancer*, Nuneaton *Hunter* and Tamworth *Mercian*. In 1980, Bromsgrove and Worcester got *Severnlink*, Cannock and Stafford *Chaserider*, Leamington Spa *Leamington and Warwick* and Ludlow and Shrewsbury *Hotspur*. And in 1981, Banbury *Ridercross*, whilst Rugby had the less prosaic *Rugby* branding.

Following the success of the VNP scheme, the system was developed to provide a scheme for the whole of the National Bus Company and was re-launched as the Market Analysis Project (MAP), which we will discuss later in this book.

Below: *Illustrating a more subtle livery change from the Reddibus scheme, No.512 (JOX 512P), was a Leyland National 11351A/1R B49F (designated N5). It is seen in Hereford town centre with Wandaward branding, introduced on 11th March 1978.* Les Simpson

Left: *The MAP scheme saw the Lancer brand being launched on 17th February 1979, and it seemed to be an immediate success. Accordingly, following public demand, a completely revised network was introduced on 14th July 1979 for the Colville and Swadlincote depots. Here we find 6015, (GHA 415D), a Daimler Fleetline CRG6LX with a H44/33F body by Alexander (designated DD12) at Coalville in July 1981. Lancer branding and operations passed to Midland Red (East) Limited at the formation of that company on 6th September 1981. However, in an endeavour to create a new image, the Lancer brand name was abandoned soon after the formation of the new company.* Les Simpson

Above: *The Hotspur MAP scheme was launched in the Shrewsbury and Ludlow areas on 24th November 1980. However, less than a year later the Hotspur operations, like the Mercia operation, passed to Midland Red (North) Limited at the formation of that company on 6th September 1981. They continued the use of the brand name, but it was soon shown on a Turquoise band with the company trading name removed. This is No.293 (NHA 293M), a Leyland National 1151/1R, B51F (designated N2). It is seen at Shrewsbury Bus Station in April 1981, with the first style of branding, red lettering on a white band, clearly obvious in this view.* Les Simpson

The Chaserider MAP scheme was launched on 31st May 1980, and based in Stafford Town and Cannock, with the reorganisation of services in those parts of the Midland Red network. It was of course to be a short-lived scheme as far as Midland Red went, for soon the services in the area would be hived off to Midland Red North. They would continue with the MAP brand names but with colour bands replacing the white band. That on the Chaserider vehicles became claret, Hotspur a turquoise, Mercian a lime green and Tellus a violet band.

Below: *The VNP/MAP area branding was mostly used on the Leyland National fleet as, by that point in time, the type had become the standard single-deck vehicle. In addition to the existing MkI types (see* Volume 3 of Buses In Colour - The Leyland National) *new examples of the MkII National were still being acquired in large numbers. One of these No.809 (BVP 809V), Leyland National Mk2 116L11/1R B49F is seen here in Corporation Street, Tamworth. It was sold to the North Western Company in June 1988. but eventually re-acquired by Midland Red South in 1997. Barry Allsop*

Above: *Delivered new in March 1983 after the formation of the separate companies, No.1706 (A706 HVT) was a Leyland Tiger TRCTL11/2R. It was fitted with a service bus B51F version of the Duple Dominant body. It is seen wearing the Claret banding in Stafford; but note the use of coach chassis specification.* Barry Allsop

Right: *Another Leyland Tiger TRCTL11/3RZ, this Hotspur No.1519 (C519 WBF) was fitted with Duple Caribbean C50F coachwork, including an on-board toilet. It was one of a trio of similar vehicles, the others being branded in the Chaserider (No.1518) and Force Ten (No.1520) identities. It is seen at the Duple factory in Blackpool prior to delivery. It passed to Midland Red South in 1987 and then re-painted to National Express livery.* Duple/Les Simpson collection

The Viable Network Project identified the need for smaller buses on certain routes. So, in July 1977, the company introduced three Transit minibuses for the new Wayfarer scheme at Evesham. However, these vehicles were found to be inadequate for the new services in Redditch. To provide a higher capacity vehicle for services at Redditch, it was decided to modify one of the Ford R192 chassis with Plaxton Derwent bodies, which had just been taken out of the fleet. As a result 6391 (YHA 391J) was shortened and the wheelbase reduced.

Above: *Seen when new and awaiting delivery No.6300 (YHA 300J) was another Ford R192, Plaxton Derwent II B45F.*
A. L. Such/Les Simpson collection

The body length of 6391 was reduced by the removal of two bays, whilst the vehicle's batteries and fuel tank were repositioned behind the rear axle to assist with weight distribution. It enteLred service on route R15 and R16 in December 1977, and it proved so successful that a further batch of similar vehicles were converted.

Over the next two years, 11 more were ordered for Midland Red's own use and three others were produced for fellow NBC operators; a further fourteen were modified including two for Western National/Devon General and one for City of Oxford. An ECW-bodied Ford was also converted for Alder Valley.

Midland Red had estimated that they could convert 20 such vehicles per year, but competition from the short-wheel-base Bristol chassis was strong, and other than those stated, no more orders were received. Of the 11 Midland Red examples, allocations were to the depots at Evesham, Redditch and Worcester. They replaced all of the Transit minibuses, and because of their more conventional appearance, they were immediately a great success with the passengers. All the conversions were from the Ford F1 and F3 classes, yet no F2s were thus modified.

Below: *Seen in the yard at Redditch garage, No.6391 (YHA 391J) is the modified Ford R192/Plaxton Derwent II B27F (designated M2).* Les Simpson

MIDLAND RED DIVISIONS

As we have seen, during the late-1970s, the NBC was still facing the dual threats of high inflation and diminishing passenger numbers. However, the arrival of a new Conservative government to replace the Labour Party after the 'Winter of Discontent', did nothing to improve the situation and it was obvious that the larger bus companies would have to look at their operations for the coming decade and expand on both the VNP and MAP concept. Indeed, the latter had been implemented throughout the whole of the Midland Red territory but this saw rural services and depots suffering heavy cutbacks and even withdrawal/closure. It is arguable that the savage pruning was to future advantage!

Above: *The Mercian brand was launched on 1st September 1979, and here we see No.6400 (YHA 499J) Leyland Leopard PSU3A/2R, Willowbrook DP49F at Kingsbury, Warwickshire in April 1981.* Les Simpson

To meet the challenges of the 1980s, and following on from MAP, Midland Red was then split in to new companies; North, South, East and West (each covering the respective geographical area, whilst Express had the coach operations based at Digbeth. We have already touched upon North, centred on Tamworth, but we must stress that it also took on the important Mercian brand, which had been launched on 1st September 1979, and seen a significant increase on the profitability of those services that were retained in the Tamworth area.

Right: *Midland Red North continued to use the Mercian brand, but later employed a Lime Green band with the trading name removed. One of the advantages of driving part-time was that you could position vehicles for photographing. Here No.399 (GOL 399N), Leyland National 11351/1R B49F. is seen at the Bull Ring Bus Station, Birmingham in Mercian livery, late one evening in January 1987. Les Simpson*

Below: *Bus operations in the Mercian area passed to Midland Red (North) Limited at the formation of that company on 6th September 1981. Three years later, in October 1984, No.6217 (UHA 217H), a Daimler Fleetline CRG6LX with Alexander H45/30D bodywork (designated D13), was pictured in Mercian livery at Corporation Street, Tamworth. Les Simpson*

Midland Red (West) Limited was another of the five bus companies created in 1981 in preparation for deregulation. It was based in Worcester, and its main areas of operation were Herefordshire and Worcestershire, along with parts of Shropshire, the West Midlands and Birmingham. Birmingham was of course served by the other companies formed from the break up of the Midland Red Omnibus Co, and all five of the new companies were to continue using the former Midland Red bus station situated at the original Bull Ring Shopping Centre.

Below: *Here we see No.656 (PUK 656R), a Leyland National 11351A/1R, B49F (designated as BMMO class N7). It is pictured at Bromsgrove Bus Station in September 1984 wearing the new MAP Midland Red West livery on the cantrail strip with the fleet name. The Poppy Red base colour is still obvious, but we should mention that West had started to phase out the local identity by 1984. Bromsgrove Depot closed on 31st December 1971, but it was re-opened on 3rd December 1973, due to the West Midland Passenger Transport Executive's takeover of other garages. Les Simpson*

Above: *Although it may look somewhat like the old NBC dual-purpose livery, this is actually Midland Red West No.546 (NOE 546R). It was a Leyland National 11351A/1R, B49F (designated BMMO class N6). On this occasion, it is pictured wearing the Midland Red West livery in Hill Street, Birmingham. Les Simpson collection.*

Right: *Carrying a variation of the National Express coaching livery, the next picture shows Midland Red West No.846 (SVJ 300S). It is a Bedford YMT with a Duple Dominant C53F body, which was not common in the Midland Red fleet. Actually, this one was acquired from Yeomans, Hereford in July 1983, with No.845 (NVJ 600R) along with the Hereford to Credenhill service. Seen at Worcester garage in September 1984 next to a recovery unit. Les Simpson*

Midland Red South and the four other new companies were all to make interesting vehicle acquisitions, and these included brand new vehicles, transfers between each other and second-hand purchases of Daimler Fleetline, Leyland Leopard and Leyland National models from various NBC companies. The new companies also acquired Daimler Fleetlines from London Transport and Greater Manchester. In years ahead, second-hand acquisitions were made from other sources, including a batch of Leyland Olympians from Glasgow.

Below: Midland Red South No.910 (B910 ODU), Leyland Olympian ONLXB/1R, ECW H45/32F seen at Stratford-upon-Avon Bus Station. Leyland had launched the Olympian chassis at the 1980 Commercial Motor Show, and production began in earnest in 1981. Seven years later, Leyland Bus & Truck was acquired by Volvo and many Leyland products were soon discontinued. Even so, because of high demand for the Olympian chassis, production then continued at the Leyland Bus Assembly plant at Workington until 1993.
Les Simpson

Above: *This Leyland Leopard PSU3B/2R with a Marshall B49F body, No.216 (JHA 216L), was one of a 50-strong batch of similar vehicles (JHA 199-248L) and delivered new in March 1973. It served with the main fleet before it went to Midland Red South on its formation in September 1981. Seen in Corporation Street, Tamworth in September 1984, after being re-seated with bus seats and re-painted into bus livery. It was sold to Ulster Bus in May 1988 and its last recorded owner was Barton Transport of Maynooth in 1990.* Les Simpson

Right: *Midland Red South No.8 (BVP 790V), was a Leyland Leopard PSU3E/4R, with a Willowbrook OO3 C53F body. It is seen at Banbury Bus Station in Midland Red South dual-purpose livery.* Les Simpson

Midland Red (East) Limited, like its counterparts devolved from the main Midland Red fleet, started operating on 6th September 1981. They took over the Midland Red bus and local coach operations in Derbyshire, Leicestershire, Lincolnshire and Nottinghamshire. Initially, Midland Red (East) Limited had an allocation of 181 vehicles taken from the original fleet, and was therefore a sizeable operation in its own right. However, the management team of Midland Red (East) Limited decided that they needed to distance themselves from, what they believed to be the tarnished image of Midland Red, which had suffered badly during the 1970s! Accordingly, the company re-branded under the Midland Fox name soon after formation, and officially re-named it as Midland Fox Ltd. on 24th January 1984.

Not only did Midland Red (East) Limited inherit 52 Daimler Fleetline double-deck buses (more than all the other new companies combined), but the company also acquired over 100 examples of second-hand vehicles from other operators, mostly London Transport, within the first few years of operation. On the single-deck front, the new organisation took on many Leyland chassis, including the Leyland Leopard and Leyland National. Of the latter, Midland Red purchased no less than 445 in ten batches, on the break up of the organisation, Midland Red East took over 121 of them.

Below: *No.245 (JHA245L), was a Leyland Leopard PSU3B/2R, Marshall DP49F. It is seen at Swadlincote Garage in August 1984 in Midland Fox livery.* Les Simpson

Above: *New to Midland Red Omnibus Co between May 1974 and March 1975, was a massive batch of 50 Leyland Leopard PSU3B/2Rs with Marshall DP49F bodies. This example, Midland Fox No.335 (PHA 335M) is seen at Lichfield Bus Station in May 1986 in Midland Express livery.*
Les Simpson

Right: *Midland Fox No.51 (XCW 151R) was a Leyland Leopard PSU3D/4R, fitted with a Willowbrook 008 Spacecar C47F body and had formerly been new to National Travel (West) in 1983. It is captured on film at Corporation Street, Tamworth in September 1984 on the X99 Nottingham to Birmingham service. Midland Fox started to use pressed aluminium fleet numbers in place of transfers.*
Les Simpson

Above: *Seen in Abbey Street, Leicester close to St.Margarets Bus Station in July 1984, is No.6441 (CHA 441K). This was another example of that huge batch of Leyland Leopard PSU3A/2Rs, with Willowbrook DP49F bodies that were designated as class S24.* Les Simpson

Left: *On the opposite side of the road is No.3147 (HHA 147L), a Leyland National 1151/1R/2501 B52F. Both this bus and that seen above are in the interim livery of dark red prior to re-paint into full Fox livery.* Les Simpson

Right: *Midland Fox purchased this ex-London Transport Daimler Fleetline CRL6, Park Royal H44/31F (which was designated as class D15). Seen in Abbey Street, Leicester in August 1984 is No.2654 (MLK 654L).* Les Simpson

OTHER SHADES OF RED

It may well be thought, with the loss of services within the new West Midlands county area, that the Midland Red might simply have been content to continue with a smaller fleet. To the contrary however, they decided to enhance their business with the takeover of several independent operators. These included Cooper of Oakengates, Shropshire on 15th October 1973, Green Bus of Rugeley on 5th November 1973, T. Hoggins & Son, Wrockwardine Wood, in January 1974 and Harper Bros of Heath Hayes on 7th September 1974. However, most of the vehicles acquired were only used for a short time.

Above: *Here we see an antiquated AEC Regent III Park Royal H30/26R, that became fleet number 2208 (BDJ 802). This was acquired as Harper Bros No.8, and it is seen at their garage at Heath Hayes. It was new to St. Helens Corporation (D2) in 1947. A. L. Such / Les Simpson collection*

Shortly after these acquisitions, and simultaneous to the transfer of so large a part of their operation to the WMPTE, Birmingham was effectively no longer the primary focus of the company's services. Therefore, on 29th March 1974, the Birmingham name was dropped from the title and the operation was then titled the Midland Red Omnibus Company Ltd.

Above: *Although many of the acquired buses were rapidly withdrawn, some of the newer vehicles from Harper Bros lasted a while in MROC service. Harper Bros 61 (SBF 447J), a Leyland Leopard PSU3/3R Plaxton Panorama Elite C51F became Midland Red No.2278. It was first withdrawn in October 1977 and eventually sold for disposal in January 1980. A.L. Such/Les Simpson collection*

Right: *New to Harper Bros as their No.25 (SBF 233), was this Leyland Titan PD2/28 with a Northern Counties H36/28RD body. It was initially used as a driver trainer in 1976, but was subsequently converted to a towing vehicle, losing its upper deck and as such passed to Midland Red North. A.L.Such/Les Simpson collection*

Above: *Another of the ex-Harper Bros destined to have a relatively long period of service with Midland Red Omnibus Company was No.33 (TRE 948L), which became a Daimler Fleetline CRL6, ECW H43/31F. It was one of a pair that were new to the independent operator in April 1973.*

Along with its 'sister' vehicle TRE 949L, it was given a MROC fleet number (respectively Nos.2233-4), and lasted in the North fleet until October 1986 (whereas 2234 lasted until February 1987). It is seen here at Cannock Bus Station.
A. L. Such / Les Simpson collection

Above: *Another of the independent operators acquired by Midland Red was the firm of Green Bus in Rugeley. It is their LJX 18, a 1958 AEC Regent V, Metro-Cammell H40/32F seen in the Rugeley garage yard. My Editor, Alan Earnshaw recalls this being new to Halifax Corporation (as their No.18) and having ridden on it on the No.43 service from Halifax to Huddersfield.* A. L. Such/Les Simpson collection

Right: *This Seddon Pennine IV, Seddon B42F was Green Bus No.22 (FRF 762K). Seen in the Rugeley garage yard. This vehicle was not only operated by Midland Red from the Tamworth garage, but it was re-painted also into the full NBC poppy red livery. Few Seddon buses have lasted into preservation, but it is now under restoration by the 22 Group.* A.L.Such/Les Simpson collection

Above: *Another of the Green Bus Seddon Pennine IV chassis was No.14 (RRE 863L), which had a Willowbrook Expressway C53F body.* A. L. Such/Les Simpson collection

The story of Green Bus is a fascinating one, if only for their eclectic collection of service vehicles. Another bus that my Editor also recalls travelling on, in the West Riding of Yorkshire, was one of the first batch of Guy Arab underfloor single-deckers with Guy-Park Royal B43F bodies Huddersfield Joint Omnibus Committee 3 (GVH 793), which was sold to Green Bus at the end of 1968, just after the JOC had been absorbed by Huddersfield Corporation after the 1968 Transport Act. Along with many other Yorkshire enthusiasts, they spent an enjoyable Easter 1969 riding around on the Green Bus vehicles.

The origins of Stratford-upon-Avon Blue Motors Ltd can be twinned with the development of the Leamington & Warwick Tramways & Omnibus Company Ltd., formed in February 1880. By November 1881, it had opened a horse tramway between the towns, using powers under the Leamington Tramways Order of 1879. In 1935 control passed into the hands of the British Electric Traction Group, and the BMMO purchased the bus operations and worked them as a wholly-owned subsidiary.

Stratford-upon-Avon Blue Motors (Stratford Blue) was finally absorbed into the BMMO on 1st January 1971, but their garages at Stratford and Kineton were retained. The Stratford Blue operating name was retained by the MROC until 6th December 1977, when the Stratford Blue company was finally dissolved.

Above: *Five Leyland Panthers, new to Stratford Blue in October 1970 were not operated by them. They were then re-painted into the Midland Red livery, again never operated, and placed in store at Adderley Street in Birmingham. All were subsequently sold to Preston Corporation in September 1971. Here we see one of the batch, Preston No.238 (AUE 310J), Leyland Panther PSUR1A/1, Marshall Camair B41D at Preston Bus Station.* Les Simpson collection

Right: *A total of 15 Stratford Blue Leyland Titan PD3s were sold to Isle of Man Road services in 1971-2. One of these No 57 (MN 57, but formerly 536 EUE), was a Leyland Titan PD3/4, with Northern Counties O41/32F body work that was converted to open-topper in 1979.*
A. L. Such/Les Simpson collection

UNUSUAL VEHICLES

To widen out the number of applications in which the Leyland National could be sold, Leyland's Bus & Truck Division decided to try some additional modifications. In years past, the low-height floor chassis produced for bus and coach applications had also been ideal for other 'mobile' vehicles that required easy access.

As a consequence, bus and coach chassis were used for mobile X-ray units, travelling libraries, dental surgeries, patient transfer, wheelchair-accessible transport, with the fitting of appropriate ramps or tail-lifts etc. and even field-hospitals. Leyland were of course well aware of this potential demand and as a consequence they exhibited at the 1974 Earls Court Commercial Show.

Above: *The 'Lifeliner' was dismantled in 1975 and rebuilt to standard service bus specifications, and it duly became Midland Red 438 (GOL 438N), Leyland National 11351/1R, B49F (designated N3). It is seen here at the last Commercial Motor Show to be held at Earls Court.*
A. L. Such / Les Simpson collection

The resulting 'bus' was designated the 'Lifeliner', and was in many ways the standard body of the Leyland National Mk3 (LSN3N), but with special appointments as well. Designed for use as a mobile operating surgery with beds for six people. An electric tail-lift was fitted at the rear for access of stretcher cases. The air suspension was modified for off-road use, and it was envisaged that a military or disaster application would be its primary use.

Above: *Being built for the Midlands, not many BMMO buses were ever sold on for further use. However, when London Transport found difficulties operating the Round London Sightseeing Tour, the operation was sub-contracted to Obsolete Fleet. They acquired seven BMMO D9 double-deckers, with most being converted to open top form (O40/30RD) at the LPC Coachworks at Hounslow. One of these was former No.4959 (2959 HA).* Les Simpson collection

Right: *Former No.5026 (3026 HA) BMMO D9, BMMO H40/32RD passed to Ensign in 1974 for use on their Lesney (Matchbox) staff transport contract then sold to St. Ferdinand Vins France, of London NW5 as a mobile wine tasting exhibition, then to Pierrots (Wine Importers) for use as a 'playbus' at Uckfield, Sussex.* A. L. Such / Les Simpson

In Conclusion

I hope you have enjoyed this look at Midland Red's Transitional Years, especially those of you who travelled on these buses in the mid-1960s to the mid-1980s, maybe a few happy memories as well. For those who have no personal recollections of the fleet, I hope this album and my brief notes will provide a fascinating glimpse into this famous firm, and how it changed so dramatically over a period of just 20 or so years. However, there is a more tangible way of examining the company's past. To see the Midland Red's history brought back to life, we would recommend visiting the BAMMOT museum at Wythall.

Above: *Well-known around the Motorcycle Speedway circuits was former No.4819 (819 HHA), BMMO CM5 C37F, owned by the Lichfield Speedway Supporters Club. It was secured for preservation in 1983.* Les Simpson collection

Here the Birmingham & Midland Motor Omnibus Trust has a superb collection of Midland Red vehicles and exhibits, details of which are on their website:- **www.bammot.org.uk**.

Of additional local transport history interest, two other museums well worth visiting are Aston Manor Transport Museum, Birmingham 6, see **www.amrtm.org** and the Black Country Museum at Dudley, see **www.bclm.co.uk**.